AN INDIAN STUDY
OF
LOVE AND DEATH

AN INDIAN STUDY
OF
LOVE AND DEATH

SISTER NIVEDITA
AND
RAMAKRISHNA, SWAMI VIVEKANANDA

GYAN

Published by

Gyan Publishing House
5, Ansari Road
Daryaganj, New Delhi-110002
Phone: 011-47034999, 9811692060
E-mail: books@gyanbooks.com

Distribution Network
gyanbooks.com
India, USA, Canada, UK, Australia

ISBN: 978-93-6920-581-3 (HB)

First Published, 1905

2nd Impression 2025

Printed at: Gyan Press, Delhi.

AN INDIAN STUDY OF LOVE AND DEATH
Author: SISTER NIVEDITA, RAMAKRISHNA, SWAMI VIVEKANANDA

AN INDIAN STUDY OF LOVE AND DEATH

AN INDIAN STUDY

OF

LOVE AND DEATH

BY

THE SISTER NIVEDITA

OF RAMAKRISHNA-VIVEKANANDA

LONGMANS, GREEN AND CO.

39 PATERNOSTER ROW, LONDON

NEW YORK, BOMBAY, AND CALCUTTA

1908

—Because of Sorrow

N.

Aug. 16, 1905.

CONTENTS

An Office for the Dead

Written for a little Sister

An Office for the Dead

To be said within the heart:

How is the city become desolate, and how lonely is now the household, that once were full of people! . . .

How is the fountain stopped up, and the lamp become extinguished!

How is our fire gone out, and how are the ashes scattered upon the hearth!

For now the hand of the Potter hath shattered the vessel that He made.

And the Mother hath hidden from us with a veil, the face of our Beloved.

Dark is the night, and terrible is the storm in the midst of the burning-ghât.

Swift and deep is the river to bear away the scattered dust.

Infinite is Time, into which hurry the passing souls.

And Love cries out in vain to stay the hand of death.

Verily are the flowers withered, O Beloved, in our forests. And all the pools are emptied of their lotuses.

For us are the voices of the singing-birds become silent, and dark clouds have passed over the face of the stars.

Since thy feet come never again across our threshold. Neither is light seen again within thine eyes.

The Salutation of the Dead: O thou that wert beforetime with us, and hast left us, hear once again, before thou goest forth, our salutation and farewell!

For all wounds and loneliness,
For all angry and impatient thoughts,
For all wherein we failed in love,
Or loving, failed to say to thee, we loved,
Forgive!
For all thy need in life,
For all thy need in death,
For labour that left thee weary,
And for love that failed to comfort thee,
Forgive!

Tenderly here at thy dead feet we make memorial of all thy past.

With infinite lovingness do we live

through again in thought thy baby-days.

One by one do all thine acts of help and sweetness and gentle self-suppression come before us.

Wondrous is the memory of our journeying together. Most holy art thou now unto us, in the presence of death.

But know, thou little flower of our great love for thee, that never, till we too are wrapped in Death beside thee, shall we forget to send thee constant aid of love and prayer.

Know thou that Love is strong as Death, that many waters cannot quench, nor the floods overwhelm it.

Thy hand is not unclasped from our hand. Nor is thy name gone out of our heart's life.

And well we know that this, our longing desire and will of love, can by no means fail to reach and give thee strength. Here or hereafter.—As God will.

But thou—dear one—rest now and be

at peace. Then waking, rise and pray with us, now and in the death-hour, evermore.

The Worship:

Thou terrible dark Night!
Thou, the Night of Delusion!
Thou, the Night of Death!
To THEE our salutation.
Thee we salute. Thee we salute.
Thee we salute.

As a man puts off worn-out garments, and puts on others which are new, even so doth the embodied put off worn-out bodies, and put on others which are new. . . .

Of that which is born, death is certain: of that which is dead, birth is certain. . . .

Never is the embodied soul destroyed. . . .

These bodies alone of the embodied Self,—which is eternal, indestructible, and unknowable,—are said to have an end. . . .

Know That to be imperishable, by

which all this is pervaded. None can cause the destruction of That, the Inexhaustible. . . .

"The body comes and goes." From Death lead us to Immortality! . . .

"Peace be to you, O people of the graves! Ye have gone on before, and we are following you!" . . .

"O great and mighty Dead! O happy Dead! The world unnumbered ages has been weeping for the dead. Weep not for the dead! Weep rather for the living, for they have yet to die!"

The Benediction of the Dead:

The Lord bless thee and keep thee.
The Lord lift up the light of His countenance upon thee,
And be gracious unto thee,
And give thee peace.
Send thee help from the Sanctuary,
And strengthen thee out of Zion.
Give thee thy heart's desire,
And fulfil all thy mind.

Prayer: O Krishna, Thou loving Shepherd of the people,
Buddha, Lord of infinite compassion,
JESUS, Thou lover and Saviour of the soul,
May Ye and all the nameless Masters of the spirit,
Visions of divine compassion,
Receive and save this soul!
Keep *her* in Thine own presence, O Lord God,
And let light perpetual shine upon *her*.

Rest in peace:[1] Speed forth, O Soul, upon thy star-strewn path!
Speed, blissful one, where thought is ever free!
Where time and sense no longer mist the view,
Eternal peace and blessings be on thee!

Thy service true, complete thy sacrifice,
Thy home the heart of love transcendent find.
Remembrance sweet, that kills all space and time,
Like altar-roses, fill thy place behind.

Thy bonds are broke, thy quest in bliss is found,
And,—one with That which comes as Death and Life,—
Thou helpful one! Unselfish e'er on earth,
Ahead, still aid with love this world of strife.

[1] By the Swâmi Vivekananda.

Prayer to Rudra:

From the Unreal lead *her* to the Real!
From Darkness, lead *her* unto Light!
From Death, lead *her* to Immortality!
Reach *her* through and through *her* self,
And evermore—O Thou Terrible!—protect *her* from ignorance,
By Thy sweet compassionate Face!

The Salutation of the Mother:

Thou the giver of all blessings,
Thou the fulfiller of desires,
Thou the doer of all good,
To THEE our salutation.
Thee we salute. Thee we salute.
Thee we salute.
Thou terrible dark Night!
Thou the Night of Delusion!
Thou the Night of Death!
To THEE our salutation.
Thee we salute! Thee we salute!
Thee we salute!

Meditations

Of the Soul

It was evening, and we sat on our zenana terrace. About us, our hidden garden bloomed, and the wind blew softly in the *neem*-tree, while beyond the roof, to the south, looked down on us the Southern Cross. At first in loneliness. Then, as the darkness deepened, it shone to the front only of a whole network of dimmer stars behind it. And then again, these faded out, and left the Southern Cross alone. For the moon was rising. And it sank, as the hours went, slowly to the West. And we talked in low tones of those who love and those who suffer, and of the seven-times happy dead. Till there fell silence there beneath the stars, and the soul watched alone:

Q. Lo, wherever I look, I behold two. To-day, life and laughter; to-morrow, death and tears. I behold joy. True, but pain is its shadow. And there, in the darkness, where I can see no further, how shall I know that my Beloved still persists?

A. Because all things bring forth their opposites. Because life is a rhythm, a rhythm of rhythms, and rhythm is but a continuous movement from one point to the reverse. Every experience within life is made up of such movement between two, and we cannot conceive that life itself should be different from all its elements. But if so, it must itself, in experience, be succeeded by death. Bodily consciousness must be succeeded by bodily unconsciousness. Manifestation by non-manifestation. This mode of acting and knowing, by not acting and not knowing in this mode.

Yet as I am myself a constant factor, in my own waking and sleeping, in health and in disease, so there must be a factor which remains constant, and undergoes this experience, of death as well as of life. This factor we call the soul.

The soul then persists.

Q. Yet, since my Beloved is withdrawn from me, even though he persist, what is that to me? Why should I not be sorrowful?

A. Is he then withdrawn? Is he unconscious? Is his persistence indeed of no avail? Let us look closer into Love itself. . . .

In life, what was it that you loved? Was it his form, his bodily presence, the sight, the sound, the touch of the house wherein he dwelt? Or was it he, the dweller within the house, whom you rather loved? Was it his mind, his spirit, his purpose, in which you were at one? What presence was to you his presence? Was it this? Or was it merely the presence of the body. . . .

Nay, the question answers itself. Grief for the body is indeed without hope, full of despair; but it is short-lived. It lasts but a little time, when the body itself is gone. It is not different in kind from the distress we feel at the loss of a valued robe or jewel. The love that endures is the love of the mind, of the soul.

If then, in life, all joy was in the presence of the soul, if the experience of the soul was the whole of love, how, in mere dying, shall this undergo change?

For the soul dwells ever in the presence of the soul. At death, a veil that confused and dimmed has been withdrawn. Shall we weep for the veil, as for the wearer of the veil?

Was there union in life?

Then, two souls were set to a single melody. And they are so set still. In this setting of the soul is faithfulness.

To the soul, time does not exist. Only her own great purpose exists, shining clear and steady through the mists before her.

To her, death brings no change. Death changes the body alone. The soul loses not her own consciousness : she loses body-consciousness. And that is all.

The cares of the body are gone. The hopes and fears and memories of the body no longer exist. But that which was the life of the soul, the thought of God, or the yearning to bless, or the burning hope of truth, remains still, gathers ever to its perfect consummation in the eternal.

In that unconsciousness of earth-life, all the experience of the earth-life gathers together, unknown to us, and finds new momentum for the renewed expression that is to come. For this is the law of experience,— impression, thought - germination, expression. And life itself is but a single complex impression, which germinates in the silence and darkness, and rises to new intensity in the next effort.

The spirit that has passed out of sight knows nothing of my struggle with poverty, of my battle with things temporal, of my toil and my defeat. No. And would I have him know ? Were he here now, is this the offering I would hasten to make to him? . . . But in supreme moments, when need or insight is quickened, so that the soul casts off her wrapping of flesh and rises alone, keen in her pain or spiritual joy, then who is to say that she felt not the stirring of her comrade? Who is to say that she was not enfolded by a prayer or a tenderness from beyond?

Look at the Catholic picture of a woman, brooding over the world, in its sin and sorrow, in eternal prayer.

Look at the Mussulman dream of a bride, setting between herself and God, as her bridal dower, the salvation of every Mussulman.

These are race-visions. And they are true. They are the great pulsations, the heart-beats of Humanity, made up of a million tiny pulses, the efforts of individual souls.

The dead do intercede, do pray, do remember us in God.

Death, then, makes nothing different.

Where the soul was, at the moment of the coming of sorrow, there it remains. And its friend and lover remains ever at its side.

All that was purely of the spirit, we share still. Grief is nothing but a clouded communion. His soul progresses still towards its own beatitude. Mine still serves that beatitude in him, and on earth carries out the purpose of his life.

Where, then, is there room for pain?

The mother watches beside her sleeping child. Does she weep, because at this moment she cannot hear his voice, cannot feel his tiny arms about her neck, cannot play and laugh and chatter with him? Or does she not rather surround him with peace and love and happy faith, knowing well that the sleep he needed carries him on to a stronger and more perfect manhood?

It may be that we, could we but see with sufficient clearness, should weep for the Beloved at his hour of birth into the bondage and limitation of the flesh, and rejoice at the moment of his release. For to the soul gone out, the memory of the earth-life must seem like a dream of impotence and darkness. And to the watcher left behind, even the body is lost, only as it is lost in sleep, or as a garment is laid aside, till it be again called for.

For still can the Beloved be served by prayer, by loving thought, by healing benediction, by charity wrought on his behalf, and by service given to the purpose of his life.

"Of that which is born, death is certain: of that which is dead, birth is certain."

Of Love

LET me commune with my own heart, and bid it tell to me again what were the tokens by which, here on earth, I knew him whom my soul should love!

Were they not secret tokens, passed by, by others, unnoticed, but to me full of significance, by reason of their response to something in myself? Outwardly, our lives had been different. But inwardly, we saw them for the same. One had led to just that need which only the other could understand. One had led to just that will, in which the other could perfectly accord. That aim which I could worship, embodied itself in him. I had dreamt great dreams, but did he not fulfil them at their hardest?

Were there not moments in which I

seemed to look through the windows of the body, and see the soul within, striving and aspiring upwards like white flame? Then knew I the Beloved, because he sought loss, not gain; to give and not to take; to conquer, not to enjoy. And I took him as my leader, and vowed myself to his quest, and knew that while I would lose myself to him, I would yield him up in turn for the weal of all the disinherited and the oppressed.

Such were the tokens, by which I recognised my Beloved, of old, and long before, the companion of my soul.

Nor is he different, now that he is withdrawn from sight. His life was as a single word, uttered to reveal the soul. The soul that was revealed, remains the same.

Much was there that the strife with earth made difficult to tell, and this has grown in him, not lessened.

That reply that my mind made to his,

the reply that was the soul of love, remains eternally apt, eternally true.

Then can I not watch and pray beside him while he sleeps, or wait to join him in that self-same silence?

Of the Inner Perception

THERE is more knowledge perhaps in simple folk-ideas of death than we often think.

For we have all known death many times, as well as life, and unconscious memories often haunt our dreams.

Like the large pulsation, made up of innumerable small pulses fused in one, so is every great and clear act of the mind, or intuition of the soul, made up of the results of countless efforts, countless experiences of the past. An irresistible conjecture is often unremembered knowledge.

And again:—

A true insight into, and discrimination of, life, is at the same time a revelation of all that comes to us outside of life. For experience consists inevitably of opposites, and the only constant is that which experiences, the Self.

Here, then, an ever-accumulating sense of weariness and loss: there, an accumulating sense of rest, and renewal of vigour.

Here, meeting followed hard by parting: there, an abiding sense of deep communion. Here, separateness: there, oneness.

Further:—

Have we learnt to discriminate with certainty the pain of the yearning that accompanies the transition from one plane of perception to another?

A pang of longing came to me for the sight of one, and at that very moment, his step was on my threshold.

My heart went out to the Beloved, in his absence, and at that very moment a letter was put into my hand, or his thought, it may be, suddenly touched mine.

Those who have watched their own experience, know this. Grief for absence is often but a veiled perception of presence.

And if there be indeed a unity in all things, then this is a consequence we might almost have deduced. For the sense and the object, the sorrow and the fact, come out of a single order, and are but two different formulations of the same thing.

What then is the message?

The message is—*Be at peace.* Peace is ever true. It is alone true. Whosoever is at peace can see truth. And he who is not at peace can see only distortion and violence.

Be at peace. For all is well, O sorrow-stricken soul, with thy Beloved!

Be at peace. For even now can thy peace serve his uttermost beatitude.

Even now can thy soul in prayer companion his. Even now canst thou fulfil his purpose, and satisfy his desire.

Be at peace. For even now, it is also true, thou hast it in thy power to shake his calm, to trouble his joy, with the sound of thy sobbing upon earth.

Think, when he was beside thee, what he was! Could he then have left thee to weep alone? Couldst thou leave him?

And now that he is stronger and freer and more himself than he ever was, could he be less tender than he was on earth?

Be at peace. Dwell altogether in that setting of the soul wherein ye were as one. For the soul, there is no time. Years may pass, but her purpose burns only clearer and brighter. Thought is eternity.

Faithfulness lies in community of soul-life.

Separation is but an austerity that passes.

When soul is one-d with soul, then is union deeper for the dismissal of the body.

Ye journey to a higher goal. In all great love, there have been many separations.

Of Peace

BUT always the wheel of Birth and Death! What then of the goal?

As long as ego remains, so long the wheel revolves. Lose ego in love. Lose love in sacrifice for others. So the Beloved becomes the Divine, and the lover forgets self.

And know thou, moreover, that when self is forgotten, then, even for the Beloved, there is no loss. For to him also, in that moment, is the Divine revealed.

Thus we cannot wander outside the circle of God's Heart, that mighty love that has revealed itself to us in glimpses here and there.

We can home to it like the soaring eagle, and the personal can become the impersonal. Or we can wait in peace, beside the empty praying-place, knowing that he who knelt there beside us once, will kneel beside us there again.

For his beatitude and ours are one. And peace is truth. And truth is found in peace.

Of Triumphant Union

——AND of that knowledge, the knowledge of the Beloved, presence and absence are but two different modes.

Either, without the other, is incomplete. For had presence been prolonged, we should have thought that presence, that companionship, was the end. But they who think thus are deluded. UNION is the end.

And union is not an act. It is a quality, inherent in the natures that have been attuned.

And that infinite music, whereby our spirits are smitten as they were harp-strings, into endless accord of sweetness and sacrifice, that music is what some know as God.

Only through God can human beings reach each other, and be at one.

Therefore must love be in restraint of sense. And separation by death is to a lover the severest of all austeritites.

It is also the highest, because it is imposed by God alone.

Pain borne with intention carries us to fresh heights.

Separation consecrated by faith reaches to deeper union.

Thus Love is crowned by sorrow. And Love, to be made perfect, *needs* sorrow as well as joy.

But when he is crowned, then doth Love put sorrow beneath his feet, and shine forth alone. And this is in truth, O blessed soul, the very Triumph of thy Love.

The Communion of the Soul with the Beloved

The Communion of the Soul with the Beloved

The Soul:

. . . LONG silence. Silence and aloneness. Yet am I sure that I am not cast out into the abyss where he is not! . . . All is so quiet. The lamps before the altar burn like distant stars. Out in the forest, the dead leaves fall from the winter boughs. The sea breaks, grey and tideless, on the long, curving shore. Only time flies, urging me ever further onward, from the hallowed moment. Fain would time make the place of parting into a shrine of memory. Fain would let die the last tones of his voice within my ear, the look of his eyes, his touch upon my head . . .

But I will not be carried! Time it is

that shall be conquered. Memory shall NOT creep into the heart, to take the place of love. All must give way, and I again walk the roadway of life in that same thought I should have known, had he not left me . . .

O Thou Ineffable Sweetness, wherein I was wont to see the face of my Beloved, rise Thou once more within my heart, that I may find him whom my soul seeks!

. . . But what is this calling-in of sense that visits me? Like ore drawn to a magnet, I sink deeper and deeper into some other state. Deeper and deeper, darker and darker it grows . . . All is still . . . Silence is His name . . .

I feel that here is the world of eternity. All is changeless, stirless, full of steadfastness. Here, earth is seen to be indeed a dream. Where, then, is this world?

Answer:

This world also is within the soul.

The Soul:

A deep satisfaction makes itself felt within me, by which I know that I must be at last in the presence of the Beloved. Yet do I not hear. Yet do I not see.

Answer:

Nay, listen! Soon will the silence become audible. Look! for the darkness is light invisible. Thou art on the threshold of revelation. Make thyself ready in great stillness.

There is quiet. In the heart, veil after veil falls. Till at last there is a great darkness. A shoreless sea of darkness. And a voice is heard, very slow and soft, as it were a throbbing of the dark:

Om! Hari Om! Infinite Oneness!
Thou art He! Thou art He!
Stirless ocean of bliss! All-containing
fulness! Universal energy!
Thou art He! Thou art He!

Secret of all wisdom! Soul of all
knowledge!
Eternal within eternity!
Om! Hari Om! Thou art He!

And the soul swoons with excess of sweetness, and in that swoon she is found by the Beloved, and awakens at His feet . . .

The Soul, speaking after long silence:

Ah! At last see I Thy face, radiant in glory. Withdraw not Thyself again from me, I beseech Thee.

The voice of the Beloved, heard within the Soul:

Come, then, little one! Let us arise, and walk with the dawn upon the mountain tops. Let us pace beneath the forest-trees at sunset, and commune.

Here, where all is oneness, is long speech, long sight, impossible. Such separateness, such manifoldness, cannot even be imagined.

The Soul:

Lo, these many days have I sought Thee, mourning, and even now know I not how Thou camest unto me!

The Beloved:

Nay, foolish one! Never was I absent from thee. Here in my heart's heart I bear thee ever, one with myself. Nay more, that knowledge unknown, that love unloved within, is the power whereby I centre myself on God, and all my being is praise.

Only thy need recalled me to the without, and broke my song . . .

The Soul:

How Thy face shines! How bright is the halo above Thy brow!

The Beloved:

It is the shining of God through the self-life. To me, thou art set in the self-same light.

The Soul:

And behind Thee, I see a great light reaching upwards, as if it would focus from above in Thee.

The Beloved:

The focus thou seest is in thine own great love. For here, and no other where, is thy ladder of light, to reach to God. Deny not thy love. Know only that separation is a dream, parting is but on the surface. Thou art in me, and I in thee.

The Soul:

Glorious art Thou unto me, O my Beloved! And yet most terrible. The strength of Thy praise scorches through all my being. Time conquers again. I am being withdrawn from Thee.

The Beloved:

Nay, each of us for the other is passing into the within. Hard upon thee weigh the superstitions of earth. Here, on the shores of Oneness, time is without power. This closeness of thy vision abideth for ever. Itself yieldeth but to a deeper possession, a more real union. Thou shalt find me ever in the presence of God. Thou art ever in mine own heart.

For thou art evermore one-d. Evermore. Evermore.

And the soul, after long sleep, arose and went about the ways of earth. And ever it knew a growing peace. For oft-times visions bring the truth, though at the first men say they do but dream.

A Litany of Love: Invocation

A Litany of Love

O Love, lifted high above all qualities
and persons!
Love, delivering from bondage,
Love, casting out all fear,
Love, in which the body has no part,
Love, eternal—transcendent—universal,
Love of the Sacred Heart, ever self-
consumed in its own light,

To Thee our salutation.
Thee we salute. Thee we salute.
Thee we salute.

Soft wings of the divine Motherhood,
Folding into their own depth and shadow
all things that cannot bear the light,
All little children crying out that they are
lost,
All error and defeat, all sin and sorrow,
All loneliness and weakness, and all unprotectedness
and simplicity of love ;
Thou the All-pitiful, folding us closer to
one another beneath Thee,

To Thee our salutation.
Thee we salute. Thee we salute.
Thee we salute.

Thou Naked Sword of Purity!
Thou, that cleavest all bondage,
Thou, Destroyer of Ignorance,
Thou, Refuser of attachments,
Thou, that remainest ever Thyself,
Supreme Love, that manifestest Thyself in Thy power, and passion is burnt to ashes.
Wondrous Equanimity, Foundation-stone of holiness,

To Thee our salutation.
Thee we salute. Thee we salute.
Thee we salute.

Thou Tempest of the freedom of the soul!
Wind of the spiritual mountains,
Insatiable longing for self-sacrifice,
Realisation of our self as all,
Love for the sake of love,
Work for the work's own sake,
Renunciation without an object,

To Thee our salutation.
Thee we salute. Thee we salute.
Thee we salute.

Love all transcendent,
Tenderness unspeakable,
Purity most awful,
Freedom absolute,
Light that lightest every man,
Sweetest of the sweet, and
Most Terrible of the terrible,

To Thee our salutation.
Thee we salute. Thee we salute.
Thee we salute.

O Infinite Love, reveal to us Thy face!
O Infinite Love, awake and abide in us!
O Infinite Love, burn us till we be consumed!
We desire not to possess Thee.
We desire not to behold Thee.
We desire to become one with Thee.

Some Hindu Rites for the Honoured Dead

Some Hindu Rites for the Honoured Dead

THE moment of sunset or dawn for the flight of souls. Sunset or dawn, and the turn of the tide. But darkness, and the silence of night, and the sound of water lapping against the shore, for the builded pile, and the flames of the death-fire!

In that Indian house where the coming of death is waited, the distant children are all called home; and even wedded daughters watch, side by side with the older women, and with their brothers' wives, for the final change. To some few, death comes with a merciful swiftness. In work, or at play, alone or amongst friends, he plucks them by the sleeve, or touches them on the shoulder, and they look into his face, and, smiling, die. It is very great, say the wise, to laugh and die! But for most of us, there are long preliminary hours of disentanglement. It seems as if the doorways of the senses had been closed, that the spirit might retreat to the inner solitude. And the man lies there, wrapt in that generalised subconscious thought that made the music of his lifetime, his body remaining passive and inert.

In that hour knows he the whole, but not the particular. He is like a traveller making ready to cross the threshold. Time wears on, till at last one of the mysterious rhythms is complete. Midnight or noon, sunset or dawn, draws near; and the fateful change is seen. The breathing grows hard, and the shadow falls. With gentle haste, the pallet is lifted and borne to a cleansed and consecrated spot in the verandah or open court—for it is thought cruel to the soul, that death should take place beneath a roof—and then, all but the dying man's nearest and dearest having withdrawn from his presence, the voice of his eldest son, or maybe a younger brother, rises alone, throwing wide the gates of the earth-life, and calling upon those of eternity to open, to the knocking of that pilgrim who stands, feet shod and staff in hand, before them.

Verily, blessed is he in whose last moments is heard no sound save the age-old Benediction of the Passing Soul:—

> "Om! Gunga! Narayan!
> Om! Gunga! Narayan! Brahman!"

A moment goes by, until, as the first of the unmistakable signs of death makes its appearance, the long wild wail of the watching women breaks forth, unrestrained and unrestrainable, and the hours of mourning begin. But some, whose distant kinship calls only for tenderness and respect, busy themselves silently to bring incense and flowers and Ganges water, that the memory of this death-hour may ever be associated in the minds of the living with thoughts of sanctity and worship. Thus, with perhaps a burning light or two, does the dead lie, in simple state, awaiting the coming of the bearers who will take him to the burning-ghât. And now and again, as one or another steals a look at the quiet face, the breath is sharply indrawn, to see the vexed record of the personal life erased, and the tortured lines smoothed out, while death establishes his throne securely, and writes, to end all things, his signature of peace. Now becomes plain the innermost secret, between himself and God, of this man's soul. Now weariness leaves him, and his main purpose, self-recorded on lips and brow, shines forth before us. Or we catch an ancestral likeness, or a broad humanity, hitherto unsuspected, even as we see the contour of some receding landscape, generalised and softened.

The women hush their sobs, and bow their heads under their white veils, crowding together, in drooping submission, in some far corner, as the bearers of the dead come in—kinsmen, or neighbours, or even hirelings, as it may be—to carry him forth, feet foremost, from the home he will never enter more. And ere they return, there must be made ready against their coming, fire in an earthen pot, and leaves of the *neem* or bitter olive. Only after touching these, may those who have served the dead re-enter their home. But all day long, thereafter, will the cup of half-burnt cinders stand in the lane beside the door-sill, as a sign to every passer-by that here to-day has death been and gone.

It has become the custom in modern times, when august leaders of the civic life are gathered to their rest, that processions of their townsmen should follow the funeral bier, with hymns and the recitation of prayers. The procession halts, moreover, at those doors with which the dead man was most familiar—his place of worship, or work, or assembly, as it may be—and services of prayer and farewell are held over him there. Those waiting at the burning-ghât to offer the last rites, can judge by the nearing sound of the singing how long or how short will be the time before the mourners—bareheaded, barefooted, and clad in white—arrive. But in the whole of Hindu music, there is neither death-croon, nor dirge, nor sad eternal lullaby. The chanting here is all of prayers, and psalms, and hymns. To Hindu thinking, there is in fact no death, and as simple folk are carried to the burning-ghât the bearers cry only by the road, "Nama Rama sattya hai!" (The name of the Lord alone is real!), or "Hari bol! Hari bol!" (Call on the Lord!), or "Harer Nama kebolom!" (Only the name of the Lord availeth!). One great measure of experience is finished. The personal, for the nonce, has found release into the Impersonal. Life has been resumed into the Ocean of Life. Our vision henceforth of the beloved dead must be subjective alone. But there is nothing here that is fatal or eternal. "Of that which is born, death is certain. Of that which is dead, birth is certain." "The body comes and goes." "Never is the embodied soul destroyed."

Many are the ceremonies to be performed at the burning-ghât. Amongst other things is the offering of the Viaticum, which, with Hindus, is given after death. A similar act of ministration will be repeated every time a requiem is performed for this man's soul; and the sight of the sacramental food will carry the mind back swiftly to the heart-piercing grief of these moments, before the funeral-pyre; so that prayers for the repose and benediction of the spirit may be uttered in all that concentration and exaltation possible only to great sorrow. Yet even now, before this *pinda*, as it is called, can be given to the dead, one is first set apart and offered for the whole world, as it were, of departed souls, "on behalf of those who have none to offer the *pinda* for them."

In this giving of the Viaticum after death, and its re-consecration at every *shraddh*,[1] the Hindu doctrine is implicit that no act by itself is of saving efficacy, that no rite or ceremony is more than symbolistic, and that all alike is to be determined and valued by its effect upon the mind. In concentration alone can we behold the truth. All that aids in the attainment of concentration is to be welcomed and practised.

One by one, at the burning-ghât, each who is present stands, to take leave of him, before the dead. In his heart, then, he calls him by his name, and silently asks his pardon for all wherein, consciously or unconsciously, he has offended him, and here it may be the priest intones the solemn farewell, "Thy friends have

[1] The *shrāddha*, or requiem, is the periodic memorial of the dead, monthly or yearly, together with prayer and the distribution of charity.

turned their faces away from thee, and thou art alone with thy good deeds."

The first brand is lighted and given to the eldest son, who goes round the pyre seven times, and then touches the lips of his father with fire, signifying the resuming into the soul of that energy heretofore made manifest in citizenship. And now is lighted the funeral fire, as the last act of personal service to be rendered by children to their dead father. As this blazes up, amidst the silence of the kinsmen, the ministering priest will recite the Vedic prayer :—

"Om !
Take Thou this man from amongst us, O Agni ![1]
By the pathway of blessed souls,
And enable him to reap the harvest of his deeds !
To Thee, O Effulgent ! is known the past of all !
Cut off from this man all his transgressions !
To Thee, O Agni ! our salutation.
Om !"

---

[1] The devotional content of this name cannot be expressed as "O Fire !" "O God, who dost manifest Thyself here, in the energy of fire !" might be accepted perhaps.

Again, hours after, as the fire dies down, are said the final salutations :—

"Om !
Now has this Mortality been merged in Immortality,
This finite soul become one with the Infinite Being.
The body of this man is here reduced to ashes !
Now, O mind ! is the time
For thee to remember thy former deeds !"[1]

This is several times repeated, before water is brought from the river in an earthen pot to quench the dying embers. The ashes are collected and scattered on the stream. And, last of all, on the spot where the fire has been extinguished, the pot is taken, now emptied of its water. A single blow is given ; and it lies, there in the burning-ghât, broken into a thousand fragments.

Human hearts and the energy of sorrow must have their way. To them a time of stern abstinence, of going barefooted, and sleeping on straw, may be

[1] This probably signifies, "Now is left to us memory alone."

devoted. But wildness and bitterness of grief is waywardness at bottom. Sooner or later, sorrow must be accepted, and the duties of life resumed.

Gently and firmly, then, does the Mother-Church deal with her children, bidding them face the world before them in a spirit of peace. Only a widow is not asked to end her weeping. To her, it is well understood, her mourning is for life. But even the daughters of the dead must go back, if they are married, to their husbands' homes. To these, three days of austerity are all that can be allowed. When this is ended, they bathe and worship. Then they make ready food for the poor, and distribute alms. Thus striving to make their loss the beginning of a new life—of deeper consecration and saddened memory, it may be, but of all the old serenity and calm—they must set forth to join the wedded kindred.

For those left behind, the remaining

period of mourning is longer or shorter, according to the degree of the bereavement. It is expected, however, that self-control and the setting aside of "the grief that rises from illusion" will come soonest to those who are most saintly and scholarly. Hence amongst Brahmins, the severest mourning lasts for ten days only.

Then is held a service which involves the communal recognition of the new head of the family. But before the household can be made ready for this, its re-entrance into the civic life, there must be a formal end to the days of sorrow. Each soul must be led to step forth from the darkness of its grief. It must be soothed, purified, and reconciled to the world and to its own part in it. Such, at least, must have been the thought that led to the composing of one of the deepest and most significant benedictions in all the ancient liturgies of the world—the Hindu Prayer for the Re-sanctification of Labour after Mourning.

Says the priest:—

"When we consider that which is past,
And that which is about to come hereafter,
We see that mortals come to a ripe end,
Like the harvests of the field;
And like the harvests of the field
They are born again once more."

And then, slowly and meditatively:—

"Om!
The winds are showering blessedness on us.
The very oceans give forth blessedness.
May our herbs and crops bring blessedness to us!
Sweet unto us be the nights and dawns!
May the dust of the earth be charged with blessing!
May the Heaven-Father cover us with benediction!
Full of blessing be the great trees,
And full of blessedness the sun!
May our herds of cattle be sanctified to us!"

Thus, on each of its children, wearied of sadness, does the Eternal Faith put forth the soothing hand of its own great wisdom and love. Indulging in no perversity of isolation is the soul called to fare forth into the great world, and tread there, manfully, the allotted path. Yet memory is not forbidden. Tender prayer has its own place. Again and again, as the set moons and the seasons go round, will the household reassemble to hear the Vedic salutations and offer rites of aid to the departed soul.

Then may arise the voice of the eldest son calling upon the spirit of his dead father, in words drawn from the Rig-Veda, and perhaps repeated on like occasions through thousands of years:—

"Go thou, and be thou joined unto the company of our forefathers,
And meet thou also with the gods of yonder world!
Ascending into the furthest heights of heaven,
Do thou receive the fulfilment of thine heart's desire!
Leaving behind thee all that has been blemished or imperfect,
Return thou whence thou camest forth,
And be united with thy shining self!

Be the gods in high heaven thy protectors!
On that path whither thou art gone before us,
Be the gods in high heaven thy protectors!
In those abodes where dwell the doers of good deeds
Mayst thou be set to dwell, by the Creator!

Like unto a traveller well-driven by his charioteer,
Who arriveth daily at more distant lands.
So mayst thou increase in steadfastness and glory!

He verily, who hath departed from this life,
Doth attain unto that other
From which death has been cast out."

And again:—

"Go forth! go forth! by those same paths whereby have gone the men of old!
By those same paths whereby must go all that are born of woman, according to their deeds!
O spirit, that art departed afar off, to dwell amongst the gods of yonder world,
We call upon thee—Do thou again return, and abide with us!

Oh thou who hast withdrawn thyself from us, travelling by the luminous roadways of the light,
We call upon thee again—Return and abide with us!
O spirit, who art resumed into the limitless universe,
We call upon thee—Return and abide with us!

Soul that to-day art departed into uttermost space,
We call upon thee—Return and abide with us!
O spirit, who art now become one with the infinite past and the infinite future,
We call upon thee again, to return and abide with us!"

Thus far, when the voice of the mourner is that of the child. But when the positions are reversed, when it is the child who has gone, and the father who performs the service of commemoration, then I have heard of a variant to the last line, and this ancient prayer, with an infinite tenderness, may end :—

"Return into our riven hearts, and there abide!"

THE END